DOOMED HISTORY

T0012308

EARTHQUAKE DISASTER!

San Francisco, 1906

by Nancy Dickman

BEARPORT
PUBLISHING

Minneapolis, Minnesota

Bearport Publishing Company Product Development Team
President: Jen Jenson; Director of Product Development: Spencer Brinker; Senior Editor: Allison Juda; Editor: Charly Haley; Associate Editor: Naomi Reich; Senior Designer: Colin O'Dea; Associate Designer: Elena Klinkner; Product Development Assistant: Anita Stasson

Brown Bear Books
Children's Publisher: Anne O'Daly; Design Manager: Keith Davis;
Picture Manager: Sophie Mortimer

Library of Congress Cataloging-in-Publication Data is available at www.loc.gov or upon request from the publisher.

ISBN: 979-8-88509-080-3 (hardcover)
ISBN: 979-8-88509-087-2 (paperback)
ISBN: 979-8-88509-094-0 (ebook)

For more information, write to Bearport Publishing, 5357 Penn Avenue South, Minneapolis, MN 55419. Printed in the United States of America.

CONTENTS

CITY OF LIGHTS

In San Francisco's Grand Opera House, people took their seats. It would be the last performance there for a long time.

The curtain lifted and the stage's new electric lighting pointed at Enrico Caruso, a world-famous Italian singer. The audience, dressed in furs and jewels, listened in awe as he performed the lead role in *Carmen*. They were proud that San Francisco could attract a star like Caruso. Little did they know that by the next evening, their city would be unrecognizable.

From Rags to Riches

San Francisco is on the coast of northern California. It was a small port city until 1849, when gold was discovered nearby and fortune-hunters flocked to the area. Even more people moved there once the city was connected to the East Coast by railroad. By 1906, San Francisco was one of the country's biggest cities. It was famous for its beautiful buildings and lively arts scene.

In 1906, San Francisco had a mix of grand mansions and simple family homes.

THE FIRST SIGNS OF TROUBLE

The **earthquake** that destroyed San Francisco struck without warning. Most of the city's residents were still in bed.

In his fancy room in the Palace Hotel, Caruso lurched awake at 5:12 a.m., when his room began shaking. He later described it as like being in "an ocean liner tossed around by heavy seas." Looking out the window, he saw buildings collapsing, trapping people under the **rubble**. The singer grabbed his suitcase and ran from the hotel. By acting quickly, he was able to escape. Others wouldn't be so lucky.

A Deadly Shake

The city had been hit by a massive earthquake. Two huge sections of Earth's **crust** had slid against each other, shaking everything that sat on top of them—including San Francisco. The quake covered an area 300 miles (480 km) long, and the violent shaking lasted just under a minute. It was strong enough to be felt hundreds of miles away, but the worst of the impact was in the area around San Francisco.

As people crawled out of their shattered houses, they couldn't believe the destruction they saw.

Many houses like this later burned down or had to be **demolished**.

Buildings Collapse

Luckily, most people were at home when the quake hit. Many of the houses in the area were built from wood, so few of them collapsed completley. However, the earthquake did tear some of them off their **foundations**. Large public buildings, such as offices or hotels were often made of stone or brick, and many of them crumbled. If the quake had hit during the middle of the work day, more people would have died as the buildings collapsed.

Keeping Order

People were panicking. Soon, soldiers from a nearby army base were called into action. They were keeping order in the streets when the ground shook again. At 8:14 a.m., an **aftershock** rocked the city a second time. Smaller quakes like this would continue for days.

The Hall of Justice, which was the city's main police station, was badly damaged by the quake.

WITNESS TO DESTRUCTION

The city's main post office was also badly damaged in the quake. One of the workers later reported, "In the main corridors, the marble was split and cracked, while the **mosaics** were shattered and had come rattling down upon the floor. Chandeliers were . . . twisted by falling arches and ceilings."

DISASTER STRIKES

The powerful earthquake that toppled buildings was bad enough. But what happened next was much, much worse.

The earthquake hadn't just damaged buildings. The violent shaking also broke the underground pipes that carried gas throughout the city. While some buildings, such as the opera house, had electricity, many people still lit their homes with gas lamps. When the pipes broke, the gas was released into the air, and easily caught fire. **Engineers** rushed to turn off the gas to stop it from escaping.

Fire!

But workers were too late. Fires had already broken out across the city and began to spread. The many wooden homes in San Francisco burned easily, sending people fleeing for their lives. As the air filled with clouds of thick smoke, ash fell from the sky and settled on the ground. The noise of the raging fires mixed with the sound of people screaming. As the aftershocks continued, buildings burned, and the sense of panic grew worse.

Thick clouds of smoke from the fires were visible from miles away.

Water to fight the fires ran out very quickly.

The Fire Spreads

In the hours after the earthquake, there were at least 60 fires burning in the downtown area. Some were put out, but others grew larger as they joined up with other nearby fires. Firefighters soon discovered that the earthquake had also damaged the city's water pipes. As a result, there was not enough water pressure to power their hoses.

FALLEN CHIEF

San Francisco's fire department had to fight the fires without their chief, Dennis Sullivan, who had been asleep in one of the stations when the earthquake hit. The dome of the hotel next door fell and crushed the station. Sullivan was badly injured and died four days later.

Cut Off

The earthquake had also brought down the wires that carried telephone and **telegraph** signals. There was now no way to communicate quickly within the city or beyond. But luckily, just after 10:00 a.m., operators managed to send out an emergency signal to the USS *Chicago*, a ship that was patrolling offshore. It immediately set a course for San Francisco to offer help.

Rescue workers raced to free people from damaged buildings.

What to Save?

As the fires spread, people raced to save their most precious possessions. For Alice Eastwood, that meant plants. The scientist was in charge of the plant collection at the California Academy of Sciences. The building where the plants were kept was badly damaged in the earthquake, and fire was fast approaching. Eastwood found a way in and climbed the broken staircase, using the railing like a ladder. With the help of a friend, she was able to save 1,497 plant **specimens** from the fire.

In later years, Alice Eastwood collected thousands of new specimens to replace those that had been lost.

Many buildings were reduced to rubble in a desperate attempt to stop the fire from spreading.

Blowing Up

With no water for their hoses, firefighters came up with a different strategy. They used **dynamite** to blow up buildings. By knocking down some buildings, they hoped to create a gap that would stop the fire from spreading between buildings and down entire blocks. Although the plan had some success, the dynamite may also have started new fires in some places.

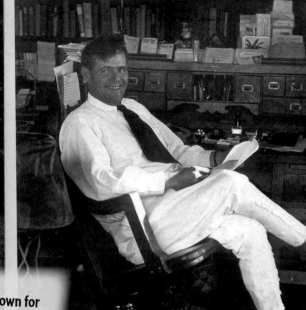

Jack London was known for writing thrilling adventure stories such as *The Call of the Wild* and *The Sea-Wolf*.

NEWS REPORT

The famous author Jack London lived near San Francisco in 1906. As soon as the quake hit, he traveled there to report what was happening. He wrote, "There was no withstanding the onrush of the flames. Time and again, successful stands were made by the firefighters, and every time the flames flanked around on either side or came up from the rear, and turned to defeat the hard-won victory."

Working Hard

Some of San Francisco's buildings survived the fires thanks to the hard work of the people inside, who risked their lives to save the city. Some people laid wet carpets on roofs and put out any small fires before they could spread. The main post office in the city was saved when some workers ignored orders to **evacuate**. They protected the building by using mail sacks soaked in water to put out flames.

The main post office was saved by a few dedicated workers.

LIFE OR DEATH

As the firefighters worked to save the city, the residents tried to escape the flames. It was a race for survival.

San Francisco is located at the tip of a **peninsula**. Because of this position on a narrow strip of land, escape options were limited. Thousands of people were able to take boats to other towns around San Francisco Bay. Others went by land, traveling south to San Mateo. On the day of the quake, the fires spread slowly at first. This gave people some extra time to flee the city.

What to Do?

Although some left, many others stayed in the city because they didn't know about the dangerous situation. With no communications or news reports, people weren't aware what was going on in other parts of the city. It was difficult to spread instructions for evacuation. Rumors spread quickly, while aftershocks were still shaking the ground. Many people decided to stay, hoping that the fires would be put out. They set up stoves and makeshift camps outside their homes, to save themselves in case an aftershook took down what buildings remained standing.

In the days after the earthquake, street kitchens became a common sight.

One eyewitness later said that he would never forget the rumbling noise of people pulling trunks along the sidewalks.

Race to Escape

The people who left the city knew that their homes might be destroyed. They tried to take as many of their belongings as possible, but the police and army had taken control of all available carts and cars. So people used baby carriages and toy wagons to carry their possessions. They even strapped heavy **trunks** to roller skates and pushed them along! The streets and sidewalks were soon littered with things that people couldn't carry and had to leave behind.

SCENES OF DISASTER

Lloyd Head was a young boy in 1906. His family stayed near their house after the quake, camping out in the backyard. He later described watching others trying to escape the city. "The sun shone blood-red through a thick haze of smoke, and people began coming in a steady steam from the district near the fire. . . . Hatless, coatless, mothers and fathers, with children all packing something, trudged on in the direction of the hills. . . . There was no water, and the noise of buildings being blown up continually startled us."

Once they had escaped the flames, many residents had nowhere to go.

Help Arrives

At about 6:00 p.m. on April 19—the day after the quake—the USS *Chicago* arrived in San Francisco Bay. A large crowd had gathered at the foot of Van Ness Avenue, one of the city's main streets. Buildings along the street had been blown up to halt the spread of fire. The *Chicago*'s crew took people across the bay to safety. Working tirelessly alongside other ships, they managed to evacuate about 20,000 people.

Once the *Chicago* arrived, city authorities were able to use its radio to communicate with the outside world.

Huge areas of San Francisco had been completely destroyed.

The End of the Road

Sadly, not everyone was so lucky. Although most residents managed to escape, about 3,000 people died in the disaster—most of them in San Francisco. Some were killed by buildings collapsing during the earthquake, while others died in the fires that burned for four days. The dead included rescue workers as well as city residents. By the time the fires were finally put out, around 28,000 buildings had been destroyed. Only 20 percent of the city was still standing.

WHAT HAPPENED NEXT

The disaster was finally over. Now, it was time for the people of San Francisco to rebuild.

Of the 400,000 people who lived in San Francisco, more than half of them were now homeless. Even those who still had places to live faced hardship. It would be some time before water, gas, and other services could be restored. People had to dig **latrines** in their backyards and get water from trucks parked on the street. Food and other supplies were scarce, and the streets were littered with rubble.

Refugees

For those who had lost their homes, life was much harder. They had lost most of their possessions, and many had been separated from family and friends, with no easy way to find them. The army helped set up tents in city parks for people to have a place to stay. These **refugee camps** housed tens of thousands of people. As the months passed and winter approached, the army also built more than 5,000 simple wooden shacks.

Tents in the camps were organized in streets with addresses. There were tents that served as dining halls and even post offices!

In the first days, people picked through the rubble, looking for lost possessions.

Rebuilding

There was never any question about whether San Francisco would be rebuilt. Just days after the quake, California's governor said, "I expect to see the great **metropolis** replaced on a much grander scale than before." Insurance companies paid out millions of dollars to replace the buildings that had been destroyed. Work started almost immediately, and within a year after the quake, there were 50,000 men doing construction work.

A PROMISE KEPT

Enrico Caruso, the famous opera singer had escaped. As he fled the damaged city, he swore that he would never come back . . . and he kept his word. For the rest of his life, he never sang in San Francisco again.

Caruso later said that his experience in the earthquake was like a "dreadful nightmare."

Building Better?

San Francisco's leaders wanted to make the city safe from similar disasters in the future. They were able to make the new buildings more resistant to fires. Unfortunately, engineers still didn't know how to build earthquake-proof buildings. And the speed of rebuilding meant that there wasn't time to test new building technology.

An earthquake in 1989 killed several people and caused a huge amount of damage.

More to Come?

The city of San Francisco sits atop the San Andreas **Fault**. This is a long crack in Earth's crust, where two giant **plates** of rock meet. It was the sliding of these plates that caused the 1906 earthquake. The fault stretches all the way down to southern California, and is still active today. There have been other earthquakes in the San Francisco area, including big ones in 1957 and 1989. And there will be more in the future.

Studying Earthquakes

At the time of the 1906 quake, scientists didn't fully understand how earthquakes happened. But after the disaster, they began studying where earthquakes were likely to happen and which types of soil would experience the worst shaking. Their discoveries helped leaders plan safer buildings for the future.

New buildings in earthquake danger zones are designed to shake and sway without collapsing.

KEY DATES

1906

April 17 Enrico Caruso performs at San Francisco's Grand Opera House

April 18

5:12 a.m. A huge earthquake hits San Francisco

6:30 a.m. A messenger arrives at the local army base with orders to send all available troops to help

7:00 a.m. The mayor orders troops to keep order in the city

8:14 a.m. An aftershock shakes the ground

10:05 a.m. A telegraph station radios a message to the USS *Chicago*, asking for help

1:00 p.m. The entire financial district is on fire

2:30 p.m. Firefighters begin blowing up buildings

April 19

4:55 a.m. All army tents in the area are sent to San Francisco

6:00 p.m. USS *Chicago* arrives in San Francisco to help with the evacuation

April 21 The last fires are finally put out

April 23 The governor of California promises that San Francisco will be rebuilt better than ever

QUIZ

How much have you learned about the San Francisco earthquake? It's time to test your knowledge! Then, check your answers on page 32.

1. **Where were most San Francisco residents when the earthquake struck?**
   a. at work
   b. in bed
   c. on the beach

2. **What were most houses in San Francisco made of?**
   a. wood
   b. stone
   c. concrete

3. **What did firefighters use to fight the blaze after the water ran out?**
   a. foam
   b. dynamite
   c. sand

4. **What did Alice Eastwood risk her life to save from the fire?**
   a. her pet dog
   b. her home
   c. plant specimens

5. **Which fault caused the earthquake?**
   a. San Andreas
   b. San Diego
   c. San Luis

GLOSSARY

aftershock a smaller earthquake that follows after a larger one

crust the hard outer layer of rock that forms Earth's surface

demolished torn down, broken, or destroyed

dynamite a type of explosive usually molded into sticks

earthquake a sudden, violent shaking of the ground

engineers people who are trained to make or build things

evacuate to leave a place because of a natural disaster or other danger

fault a long break in the rock of Earth's surface, where earthquakes can sometimes happen

foundations the lowest parts of a building, often below ground level, which support the weight of the rest of the building

latrines simple toilets in a camp used by a number of people

metropolis a large, important city

mosaics decorations on a surface made by arranging small pieces of differently colored glass, tile, or stone to form pictures or patterns

peninsula a piece of land that sticks out into a body of water that almost completely surrounds it

plates slabs of rock that make up Earth's surface; the places where they meet often have earthquakes and volcanoes

refugee camps temporary camps where people who have been forced to leave their homes can take shelter

rubble rough pieces of stone, brick, and concrete that are broken off damaged buildings

specimens plants, animals, rocks, or other natural objects used for scientific study

telegraph an old system for sending messages long distances, using electrical pulses sent over metal wires

trunks large, strong cases used for storing things or for taking them on long journeys

INDEX

READ MORE

Bybee, Veeda. *Lily and the Great Quake: A San Francisco Earthquake Survival Story (Girls Survive).* North Mankato, MN: Stone Arch Books, 2020.

Collins, Ailynn. *Can You Survive the Great San Francisco Earthquake? An Interactive History Adventure (You Choose: Disasters in History).* North Mankato, MN: Capstone Press, 2022.

Loh-Hagan, Virginia. *When the Ground Shook: San Francisco Earthquake of 1906 (Behind the Curtain).* Ann Arbor, MI : Cherry Lake Publishing, 2020.

LEARN MORE ONLINE

1. Go to **www.factsurfer.com** or scan the QR code below.

2. Enter **"Earthquake Disaster "** into the search box.

3. Click on the cover of this book to see a list of websites.

Answers to the quiz on page 30
1) B; 2) A; 3) B; 4) C; 5) A